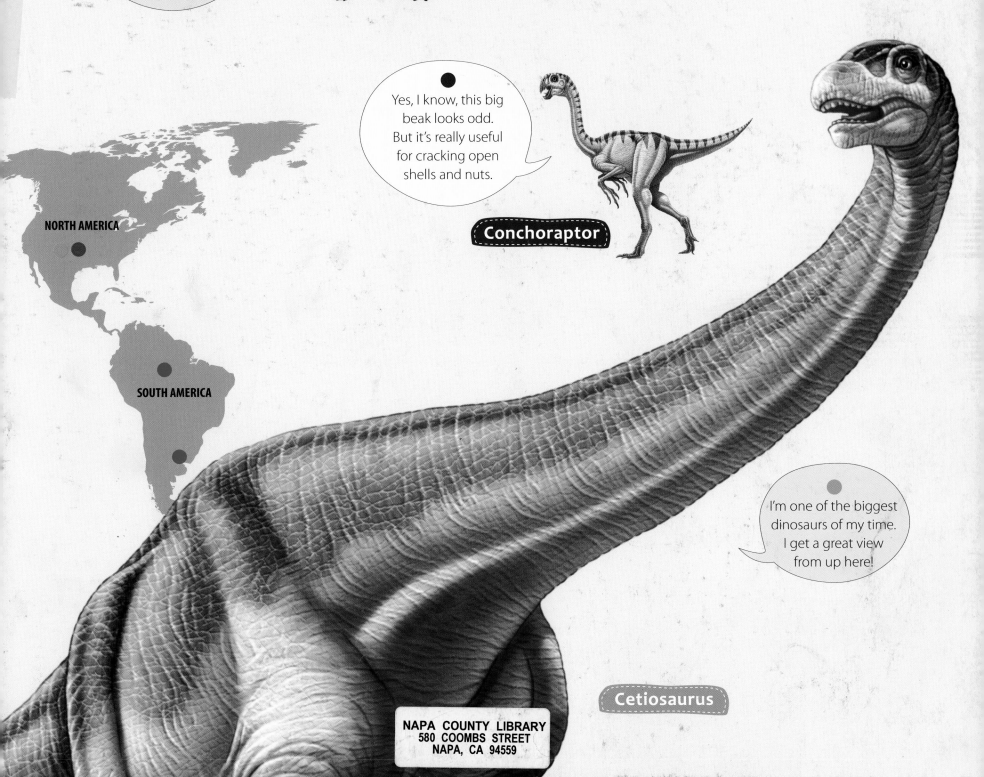

big & SMALL

Original Korean text and illustrations by Dreaming Tortoise
Korean edition © Aram Publishing

This English edition published by big & SMALL in 2017
by arrangement with Aram Publishing
English text edited by Scott Forbes
English edition © big & SMALL 2017

Distributed in the United States and Canada by
Lerner Publishing Group, Inc.
241 First Avenue North
Minneapolis, MN 55401 U.S.A.
www.lernerbooks.com

Photo credits:
Page 28, center: © Kabacchi
Page 29, center: © Kabacchi

ISBN: 978-1-925235-22-7
Printed in Korea

To learn more about dinosaur fossils, see page 28.
For information on the main groups of dinosaurs,
see the Dinosaur Family Tree on page 30.

Restless
Iguanodon

Iguanodon

big & SMALL

Protoceratops

SAY IT:
Pro-toh-SER-ah-tops

First the Protoceratops heard the thump of heavy footsteps. Then they saw the giant creature approaching — a deadly Tarbosaurus. The mother Protoceratops began to cover her eggs with dirt, trying to hide them.

TARBOSAURUS

GROUP: Theropods
DIET: Meat
WHEN IT LIVED: Late Cretaceous
WHERE IT LIVED: Asia (Mongolia, China)
LENGTH: 40–43 feet (12–13 meters)
HEIGHT: 16.5 feet (5 meters)
WEIGHT: 6.6–7.7 tons
(6–7 tonnes)

Protoceratops was an early ancestor of the horned dinosaurs, or ceratopsians, and its name means "first horned face." However, it had only small cheek horns. Its large beak-like jaw contained lots of strong teeth for chewing tough plants.

HEIGHT: 3.3 feet
(1 meter)

LENGTH: 5–6.6 feet
(1.5–2 meters)

WEIGHT: 530 pounds
(240 kilograms)

WHEN IT LIVED:	TRIASSIC	JURASSIC	CRETACEOUS
GROUP: Ceratopsians		DIET: Plants	

WHERE IT LIVED:
Asia (Mongolia, China, South Korea)

Fortunately, the Tarbosaurus was distracted
by other prey. The Protoceratops were very relieved.
They waited till they thought it was entirely safe, then
moved away from the nest to feed on some nearby plants.
But as they were doing that, a pair of Oviraptors appeared!

8

The Oviraptors dashed toward the nest. The Protoceratops were too small to fight them off. They could only watch as the Oviraptors made off with a couple of their eggs.

Fortunately, there were still several eggs in the nest and the mother Protoceratops would soon lay more. At least some of its babies were likely to survive.

OVIRAPTOR

GROUP: Theropods
DIET: Meat
WHEN IT LIVED: Late Cretaceous
WHERE IT LIVED: Asia (Mongolia, China)
LENGTH: 6.6 feet (2 meters)
HEIGHT: 2.6 feet (0.8 meters)
WEIGHT: 77–88 pounds
(35–40 kilograms)

Staurikosaurus

SAY IT:
Staw-ree-koh-SAW-rus

The Staurikosaurus had been hunting all morning and had found no food at all. They had wandered far from their usual hunting ground. They were just about to give up and have a rest when they saw a lizard darting through some nearby rocks. Quick as a flash, one of the Staurikosaurus snatched it up.

Staurikosaurus was a small dinosaur. But it was fast and fierce, and it often hunted in packs. So it was usually good at catching prey.

Staurikosaurus means "Southern Cross Lizard." The Southern Cross is a group of stars that is visible only in the Southern Hemisphere, where this dinosaur lived.

As the Staurikosaurus began to eat the lizard, they heard a loud roaring behind them. When they turned around, they found themselves face to face with a fearsome Herrerasaurus. Clearly this was its hunting ground! Fortunately, the Staurikosaurus were fast runners, and they soon escaped — taking the lizard with them!

Staurikosaurus' light body and strong back legs helped it run fast and turn quickly. Its teeth were long and sharp, and it fed mainly on lizards, small mammals, and insects.

HERRERASAURUS

GROUP: Theropods
DIET: Meat
WHEN IT LIVED: Late Triassic
WHERE IT LIVED: South America (Argentina)
LENGTH: 10–16 feet (3–5 meters)
HEIGHT: 3.6 feet (1.1 meters)
WEIGHT: 460–770 pounds (210–350 kilograms)

HEIGHT: 2.6 feet (80 centimeters)
LENGTH: 6.6 feet (2 meters)
WEIGHT: 66 pounds (30 kilograms)

WHEN IT LIVED: | TRIASSIC | JURASSIC | CRETACEOUS

GROUP: Theropods
DIET: Meat
WHERE IT LIVED: South America (Brazil, Argentina)

Garudimimus

SAY IT:
Gah-roo-deh-MY-mus

The Garudimimus crept toward the Bagaceratops' nest. Hidden behind a rock, they waited until the Bagaceratops wandered off in search of food, then they dashed to the nest. They snatched up the eggs and fled in all directions.

BAGACERATOPS

GROUP: Ceratopsia
DIET: Plants
WHEN IT LIVED: Late Cretaceous
WHERE IT LIVED: Asia (Mongolia)
LENGTH: 3.3 feet (1 meter)
HEIGHT: 1.6 feet (0.5 meters)
WEIGHT: 20 pounds
(9 kilograms)

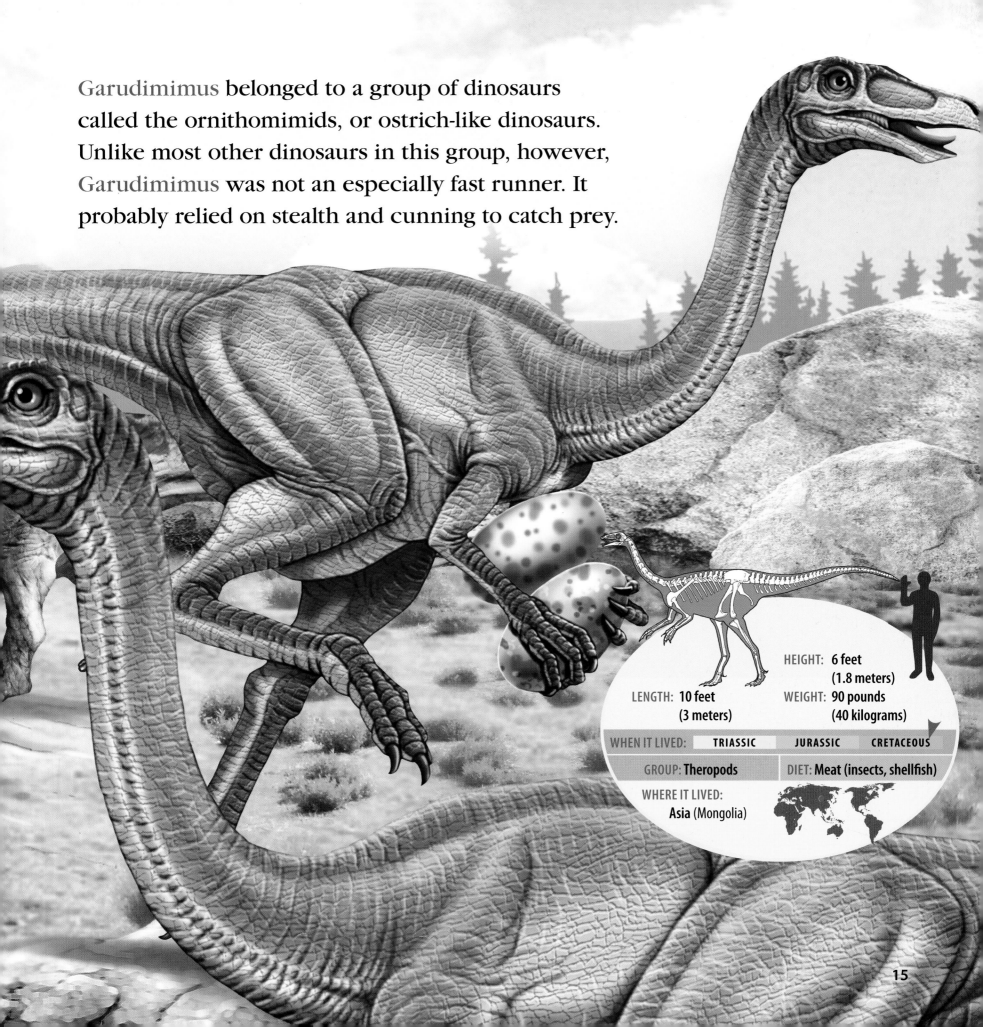

Garudimimus belonged to a group of dinosaurs called the ornithomimids, or ostrich-like dinosaurs. Unlike most other dinosaurs in this group, however, Garudimimus was not an especially fast runner. It probably relied on stealth and cunning to catch prey.

LENGTH: **10 feet** (3 meters)

HEIGHT: **6 feet** (1.8 meters)

WEIGHT: **90 pounds** (40 kilograms)

WHEN IT LIVED: TRIASSIC JURASSIC CRETACEOUS

GROUP: **Theropods**

DIET: **Meat (insects, shellfish)**

WHERE IT LIVED: **Asia** (Mongolia)

Cetiosaurus

SAY IT:
See-tee-oh-SAW-rus

The Cetiosaurus saw the Allosaurus approach. They quickly moved in front of their young and prepared to defend them to the death.

ALLOSAURUS

GROUP: Theropods
DIET: Meat
WHEN IT LIVED: Late Jurassic
WHERE IT LIVED: North America (USA), Europe (Portugal), Africa (Tanzania), Australia
LENGTH: 25–40 feet (7.5–12 meters)
HEIGHT: 10–13 feet (3–4 meters)
WEIGHT: 1.6–3.3 tons (1.5–3 tonnes)

The Allosaurus circled around the giant plant-eaters, looking for a chance to dart in and snatch up the young Cetiosaurus. But any time they got close, the adults lashed out at them with their massive, whip-like tails.

The Cetiosaurus kept driving the Allosaurus away.
They were determined to protect their young.
Battered by the Cetiosaurus' tails, the Allosaurus soon
grew tired and ran off in search of easier prey.

HEIGHT: **16 feet**
(5 meters)

LENGTH: **50 feet**
(15 meters)

WEIGHT: **12.1 tons**
(12 tonnes)

WHEN IT LIVED: **TRIASSIC** | **JURASSIC** | **CRETACEOUS**

GROUP: **Sauropods**

DIET: **Plants**

WHERE IT LIVED:
North America (America),
Africa (Morocco),
Europe

Cetiosaurus means "sea monster lizard." It was given this name because when fossils of this dinosaur were first discovered scientists thought they might belong to a giant sea creature.

Conchoraptor

SAY IT:
CON-co-rap-tor

Down on the lakeshore, the water level had dropped. Scattered across the exposed sands were dozens of big shells.

A group of Conchoraptors rushed down to the shore.
They began to use their strong, beak-like jaws to break
open the shells and feed on the creatures inside.
What a feast!

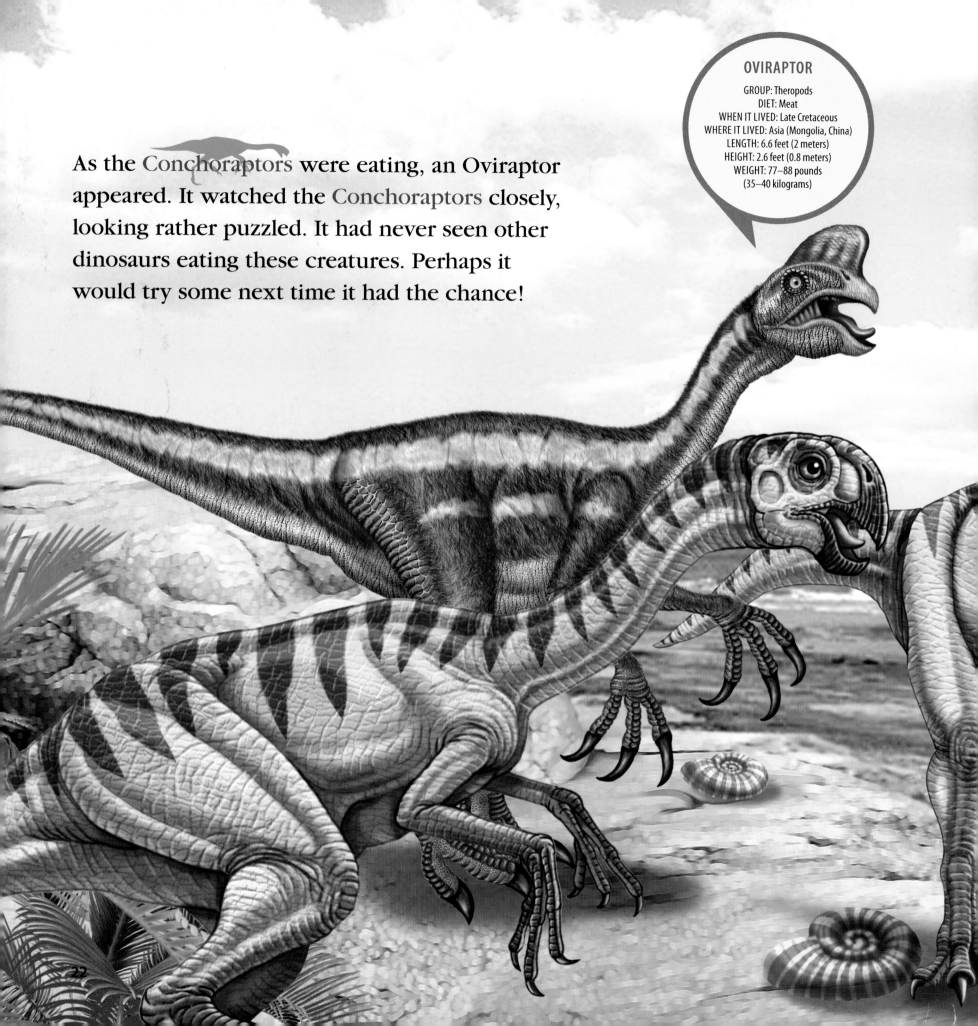

As the Conchoraptors were eating, an Oviraptor appeared. It watched the Conchoraptors closely, looking rather puzzled. It had never seen other dinosaurs eating these creatures. Perhaps it would try some next time it had the chance!

OVIRAPTOR

GROUP: Theropods
DIET: Meat
WHEN IT LIVED: Late Cretaceous
WHERE IT LIVED: Asia (Mongolia, China)
LENGTH: 6.6 feet (2 meters)
HEIGHT: 2.6 feet (0.8 meters)
WEIGHT: 77–88 pounds
(35–40 kilograms)

LENGTH: 3.3–6.6 feet
(1–2 meters)

HEIGHT: 2.6 feet
(0.8 meters)

WEIGHT: 33 pounds
(15 kilograms)

WHEN IT LIVED:	TRIASSIC	JURASSIC	CRETACEOUS
GROUP: **Theropods**		DIET: **Meat**	

WHERE IT LIVED:
Asia (Mongolia)

Conchoraptor means "conch thief." A conch is a large shell. Conchoraptors did not have teeth, but their strong beaks were ideal for breaking open shells, and may also have been used for opening nuts and snails.

Iguanodon

SAY IT:
Ig-WAH-no-don

The mother Iguanodon raised her head and listened.
She sensed something large approaching.
At once she signaled to her young, who were
busy feeding on leaves, to get ready to move on.
Clearly, this place was no longer safe.

24

Iguanodon was a large, gentle dinosaur that fed on plants. It lived in large groups, or herds, which constantly traveled around, looking for food.

Iguanodon had many rows of teeth inside its mouth, and could chew through large quantities of plants.

Just as the Iguanodons were about to move off,
a fearsome meat-eating dinosaur, Neovenator,
appeared. The young Iguanodons cowered close
to the ground. But the mother stepped forward
and swung at the Neovenator with her huge, spiked
thumb claws. Fighting frantically, she managed to
drive the Neovenator away and keep her young safe.

Iguanodon usually walked on four legs, but it could rise up on its back legs to run faster or to reach high branches. Standing up on its back legs also made it look bigger, which may have helped it scare off attackers.

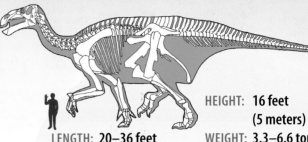

LENGTH: 20–36 feet (6–11 meters)

HEIGHT: 16 feet (5 meters)

WEIGHT: 3.3–6.6 tons (3–6 tonnes)

WHEN IT LIVED: TRIASSIC | JURASSIC | CRETACEOUS

GROUP: Ornithopods

DIET: Plants

WHERE IT LIVED: North America, Asia (Mongolia), Europe (England, Germany), Africa (Tunisia)

NEOVENATOR

GROUP: Theropods
DIET: Meat
WHEN IT LIVED: Early Cretaceous
WHERE IT LIVED: Europe (England)
LENGTH: 26 feet (8 meters)
HEIGHT: 8 feet (2.5 meters)
WEIGHT: 0.8 tons (750 kilograms)

Dinosaur Fossils

Fossils are the remains of dinosaurs. They can be hard parts of dinosaurs, such as bones and teeth, that have slowly turned to stone. Or they may be impressions of bones, teeth, or skin preserved in rocks.

▲ Model of a Protoceratops skeleton

Protoceratops

In 1922, an American expedition to Mongolia, led by dinosaur hunter Roy Chapman Andrews, discovered the first fossils of Protoceratops, including a nest and eggs. A fossil of an Oviraptor was found nearby, and it was assumed that the Oviraptor was trying to steal the Protoceratops' eggs. However, scientists now think the Oviraptor was protecting its own eggs. A later Protoceratops fossil, unearthed in 1965, is one of the only fossils to be found with a matching fossilized footprint.

Staurikosaurus

Staurikosaurus is one of the earliest known dinosaurs, alongside Eoraptor and Herrerasaurus. The first Staurikosaurus fossils were found in southern Brazil in 1970. Staurikosaurus had a long tail with more than 40 bones. Studies show it held its tail out straight as it ran, probably using it to help it keep its balance and change direction.

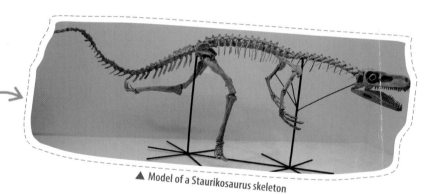

▲ Model of a Staurikosaurus skeleton

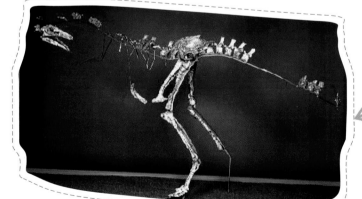

▲ Model of a Garudimimus skeleton

Garudimimus

The first Garudimimus fossil was discovered in 1981, in southern Mongolia. It is thought to have been one of the so-called ostrich-like dinosaurs, but unlike most dinosaurs in that group it had four toes rather than three and heavier legs, which probably meant it wasn't a very fast runner. Garudimimus is named for the Garuda, a famous winged creature from Buddhist mythology.

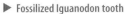
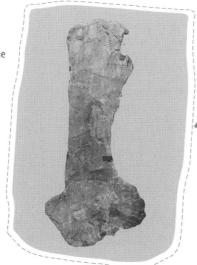

Cetiosaurus

Cetiosaurus was the first of the giant plant-eating dinosaurs known as sauropods to be discovered, in 1825 in England. Initially, scientists thought the bones belonged to a huge sea creature. The famous scientist Sir Richard Owen, who coined the term "dinosaur," gave Cetiosaurus its name in 1841. But it was not until 1869, 28 years after its discovery, that the fossil was recognized as a dinosaur fossil.

Conchoraptor

When dinosaur hunters found fossils of Conchoraptor in Mongolia's Gobi Desert in 1971, they thought they were the bones of a baby Oviraptor. The fossils lacked the Oviraptor's usual crest, but the scientists thought this was simply because the dinosaur was young and hadn't had time to grow a crest before it died. Thirty years later, however, studies showed that the fossils belonged to a different, smaller dinosaur, which was then given the name Conchoraptor.

▲ Model of a Conchoraptor skeleton

▶ Fossilized Iguanodon tooth

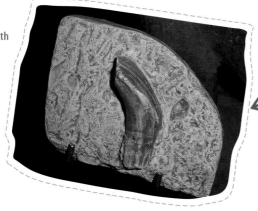

Iguanodon

While exploring a quarry in southern England in 1822, Dr. Gideon Mantell found the first Iguanodon fossils — several teeth. He realized they were similar to those of an iguana, so he gave the creature the name Iguanodon, meaning "iguana tooth." Later, Mantell found more Iguanodon fossils, including a thumb claw, which he thought was a horn from the creature's nose. He then worked out that the Iguanodon had to have been more than 100 feet (30 meters) long.

THE DINOSAUR FAMILY TREE

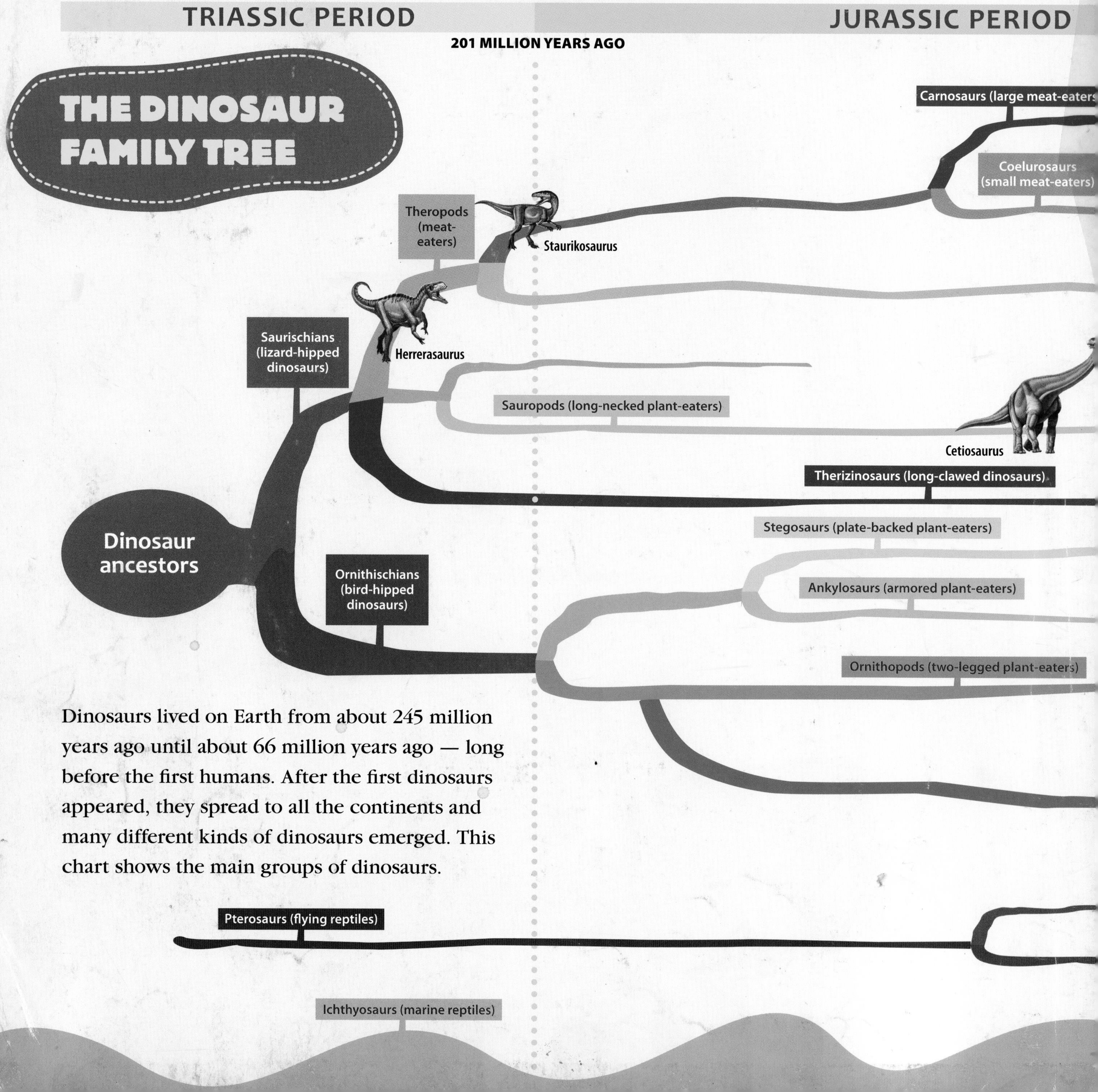

TRIASSIC PERIOD
JURASSIC PERIOD
201 MILLION YEARS AGO
Carnosaurs (large meat-eaters
Coelurosaurs (small meat-eaters)
Theropods (meat-eaters)
Staurikosaurus
Herrerasaurus
Saurischians (lizard-hipped dinosaurs)
Sauropods (long-necked plant-eaters)
Cetiosaurus
Therizinosaurs (long-clawed dinosaurs)
Dinosaur ancestors
Stegosaurs (plate-backed plant-eaters)
Ornithischians (bird-hipped dinosaurs)
Ankylosaurs (armored plant-eaters)
Ornithopods (two-legged plant-eaters)
Pterosaurs (flying reptiles)
Ichthyosaurs (marine reptiles)

Dinosaurs lived on Earth from about 245 million years ago until about 66 million years ago — long before the first humans. After the first dinosaurs appeared, they spread to all the continents and many different kinds of dinosaurs emerged. This chart shows the main groups of dinosaurs.